The Medium Maze Activity Book for Cat Lovers!

25 Medium Maze Puzzles with Answer Keys!

By J.L.W.

Help the cat follow the path to reach the goal.
Trace the path with your finger or pencil.
Avoid the dead ends. Ready? Meow, let's go!

Thank you for your support! Your purchase directly helps
Kawakuji Animal Rescue and Fruits Basket Fosters save and
care for cats and kittens in Japan. Together, we're committed
to finding loving homes for those in need. Your kindness
makes a pawsitive impact!
**Disclaimer, we are not artists and as such the pictures in
this maze book will not impress or amaze you. Please don't
let our terrible doodles we draw while fostering cats and
kittens distract from the mazes. Thank you.**
©FruitsBasketFosters 2023

1

Guide the cat to a fishy feast!

2

Lead the cat to its cozy bed.

Help the cat find its favorite toy.

Guide the cat to a tasty treat.

Help the cat find its soft blanket.

Guide the cat to a ball of yarn.

Lead the cat to a bunch of catnip.

Help the cat find its hidden mouse.

Guide the cat to a napping spot.

Lead the cat to its scratching post.

Help the cat find its ball toy.

Help the cat find its cozy window.

Help the cat find its comfy cushion.

Lead the cat to a sunny spot.

16

Guide the cat to its yummy dinner.

Guide the cat to a clean litter box.

Help the cat catch a pesky mouse.

Lead the cat to a cool hat.

Guide the cat to a comfy couch.

Help the cat get some fresh water.

Lead the cat to its favorite collar.

Guide the cat to a bird toy.

Lead the cat to a fun wand toy.

Help the cat find its forever home.

ANSWER KEY!

Fun fact! These mazes are all drawn by hand while the Fruits Basket Fosters hang out in their foster room. It's a quiet activity that allows the kittens and cats a good opportunity to explore their new surroundings and meet their new foster parents without fear! All of the cat drawings are actual poses previous fosters have been in while their foster parents watched over them! Check out @FruitsBasketFosters on instagram for tons of adorable cat and kitten photos!

27

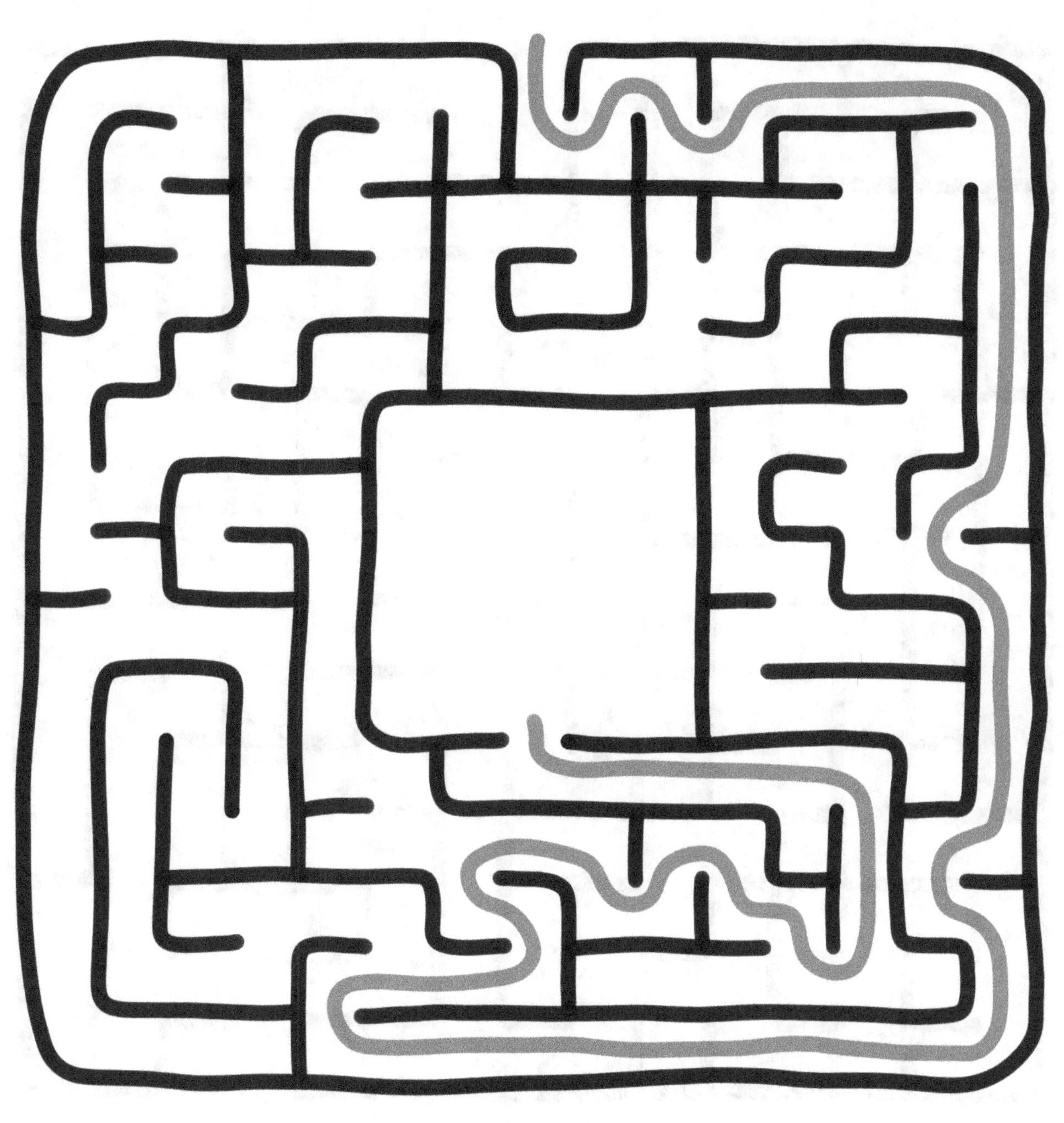

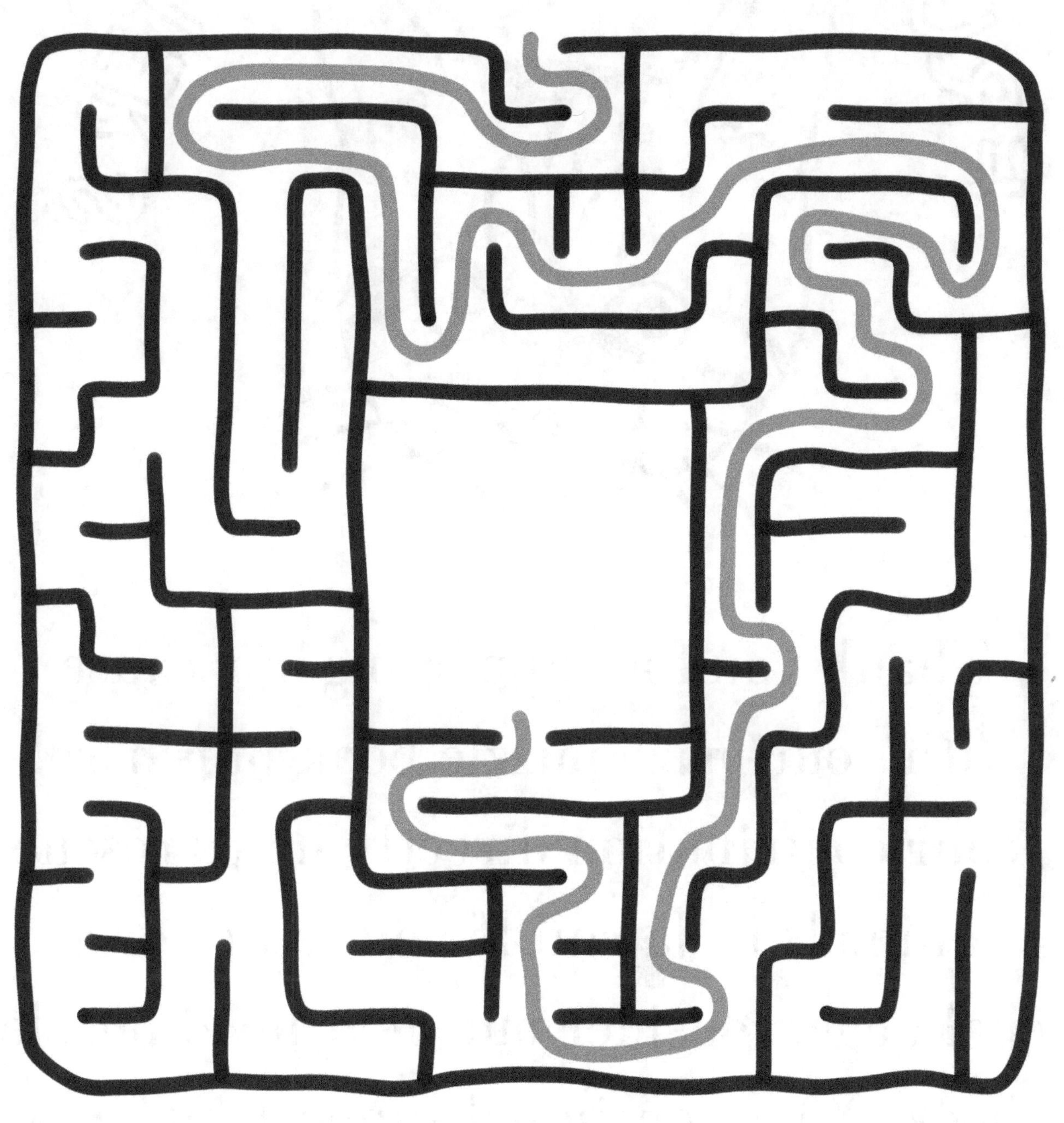

Thank you for supporting our cause with your maze puzzle book purchase! Your contribution directly helps rescue animals in Japan! If you're up for a challenge, consider our next level puzzle book. Your continued support makes a difference. Keep puzzling and purring!